PIANO SOLO

BATTLESTAR
GALACTICA

MUSIC BY
BEAR McCREARY

ISBN 978-1-61780-367-3

HAL•LEONARD®
CORPORATION
7777 W. BLUEMOUND RD. P.O. BOX 13819 MILWAUKEE, WI 53213

Visit Hal Leonard Online at
www.halleonard.com

CONTENTS

A NOTE FROM THE COMPOSER

My score to *Battlestar Galactica* is known for its pounding taiko drums, wailing ethnic soloists and Middle Eastern-inspired heavy metal guitar riffs. However, the solo piano has always been an important instrument in the score. While relegated to the background at first, the piano gradually worked its way to the foreground, culminating with "Someone to Watch Over Me." In this crucial episode, Kara Thrace actually plays the piano and learns the music that proves pivotal to the resolution of the series. I wrote music after reading the script and was on set, teaching the actors to play and supervising the creation of the music. The piano had broken free from the score and was now actually a character on screen!

The solo piano pieces featured in that episode, notably "Dreilide Thrace Sonata No. 1" and "Elegy," are among the strongest compositions I ever created for the show. As I prepared them for publication, I realized many other "Galactica" compositions would translate well to piano. Having performed suites of this score live in concerts with the Battlestar Galactica Orchestra, I already knew this music had a life of its own outside the television series. At last, fans can now be a part of the musical process themselves and experience the score as I first did: with fingertips touching the ivories.

I have personally arranged each of these pieces, ensuring the ideal translation from orchestral score to solo piano. Special thanks are due to Charmaine Siagian and everyone at Hal Leonard Corporation for their attention to detail and enthusiasm for bringing the music of *Battlestar Galactica* to pianists everywhere. So Say We All!

Bear McCreary
Los Angeles
December 2010

Roslin and Adama

By Bear McCreary

Simple Folk feel (♩ = 88)

p

Pedal freely

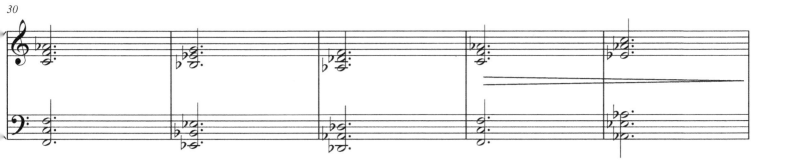

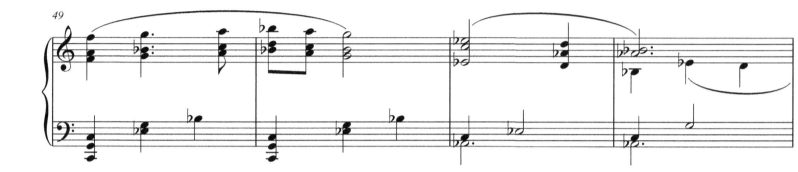

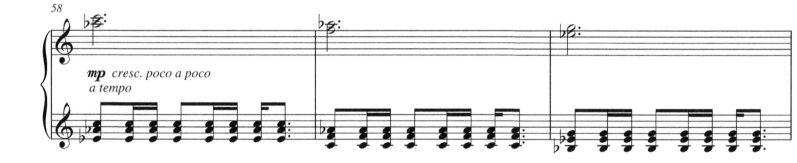

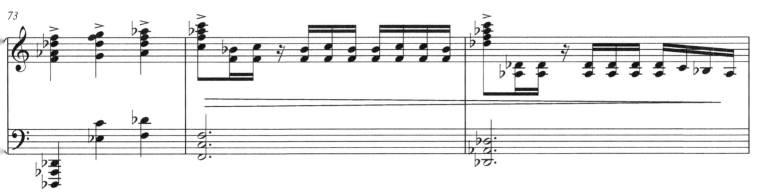

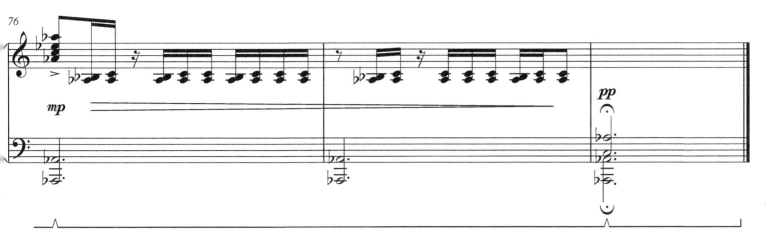

Wander My Friends

By Bear McCreary

Pedal freely

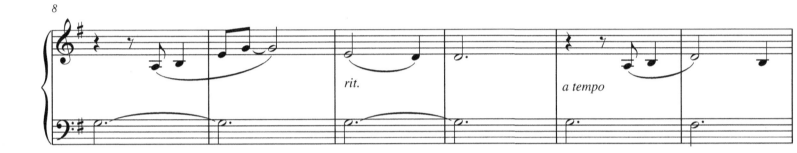

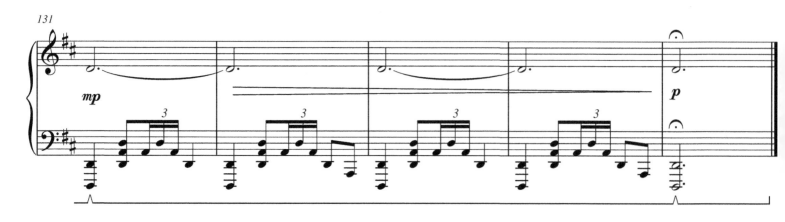

Passacaglia

By Bear McCreary

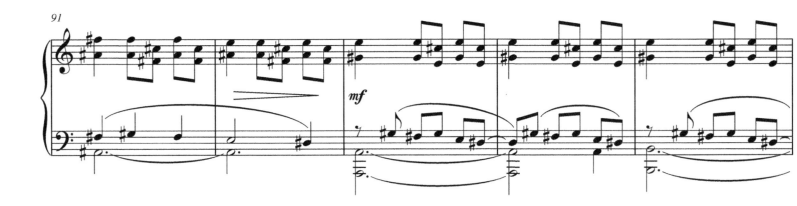

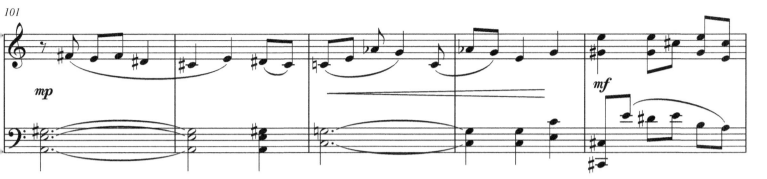

The Shape of Things to Come

By Bear McCreary

Steady, with building energy (♩. = 66)

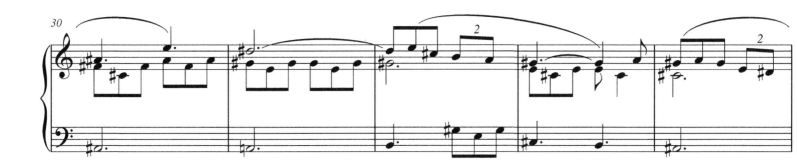

43

48

54

59

64

22

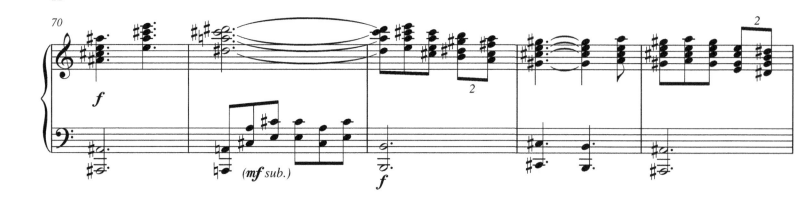

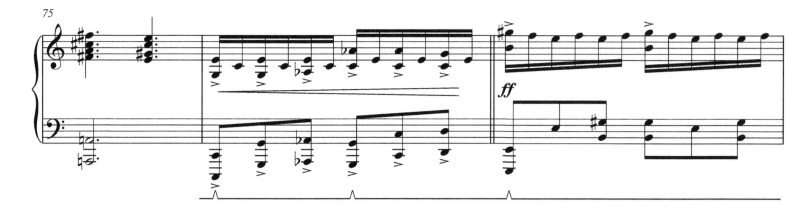

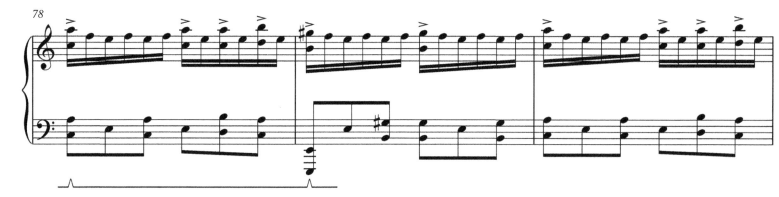

Dreilide Thrace Sonata No. 1

By Bear McCreary

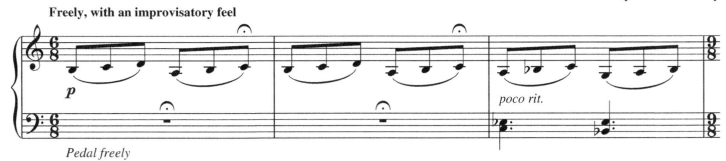

24

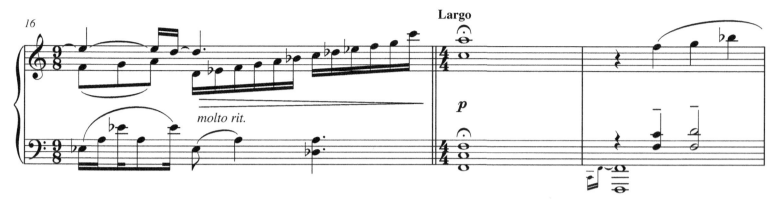

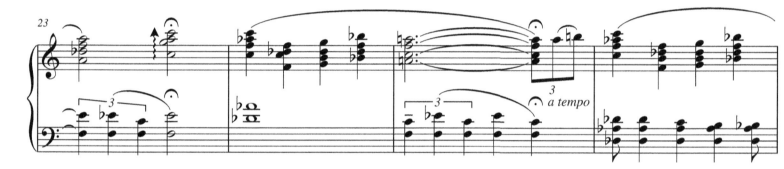

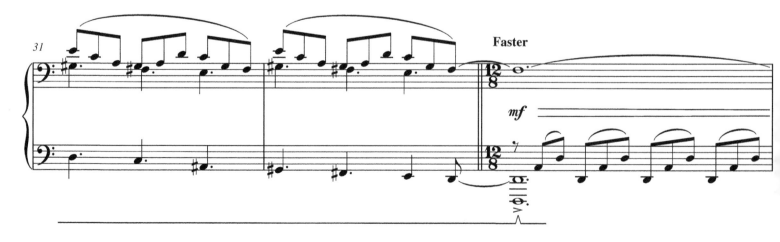

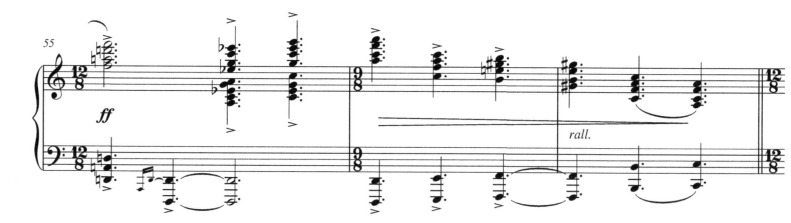

Cadenza, freely

28

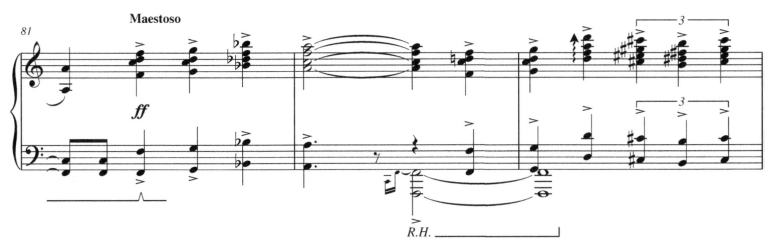

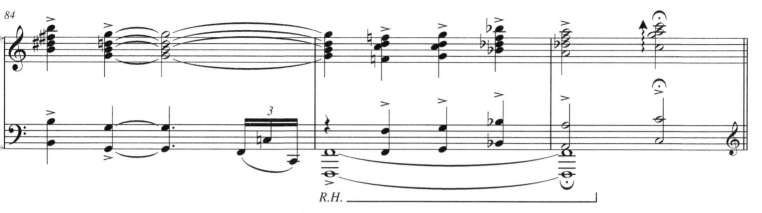

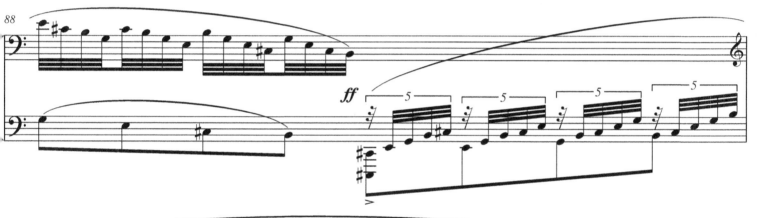

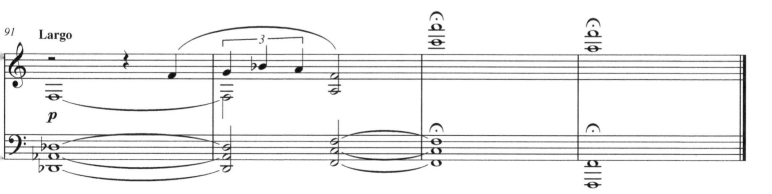

Elegy

By Bear McCreary

Molto rubato, with an improvisatory feel (♩. = 74)

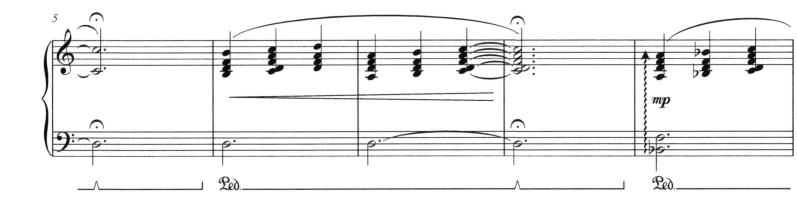

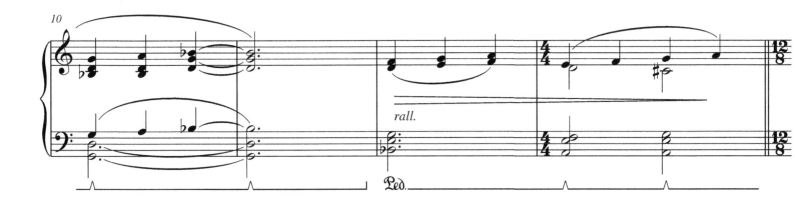

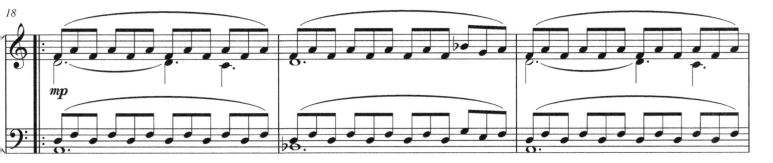

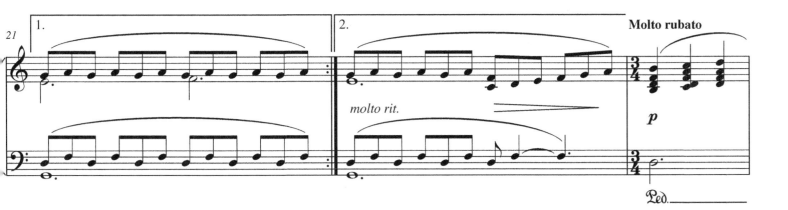

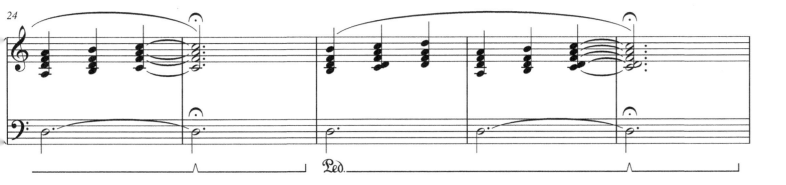

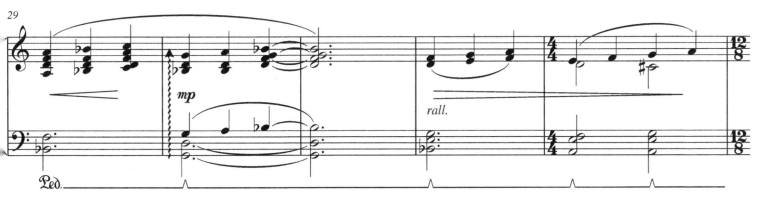

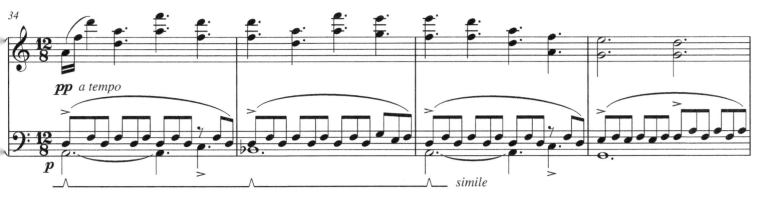

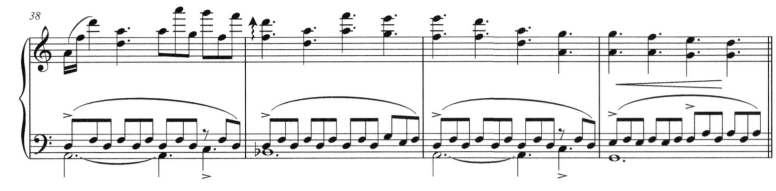

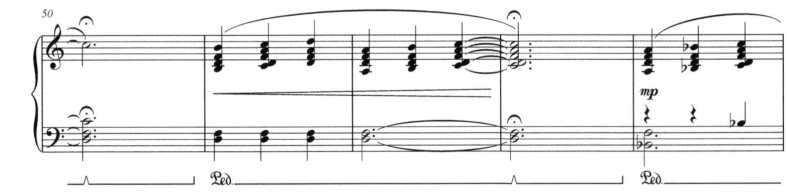

Battlestar Sonatica

By Bear McCreary

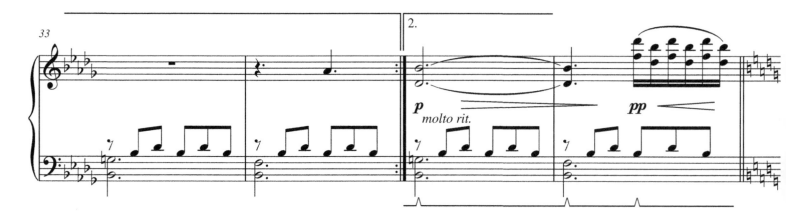

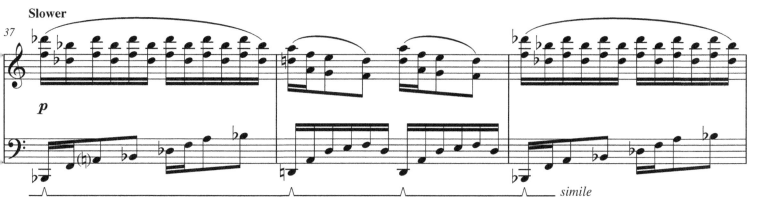

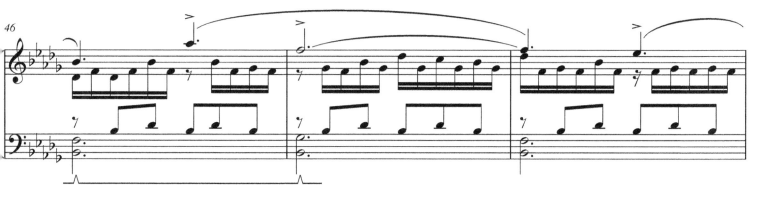

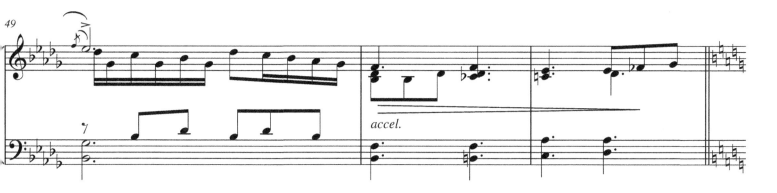

Tempo Primo

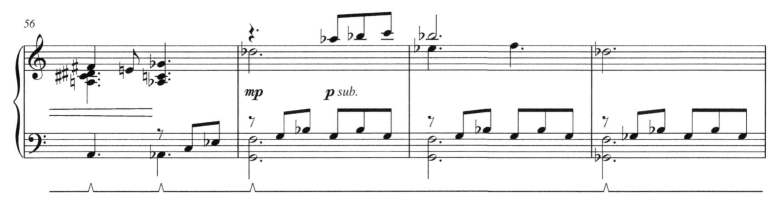

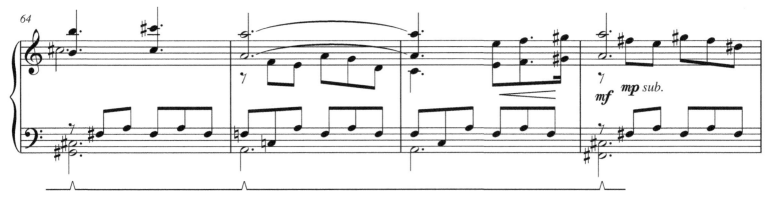

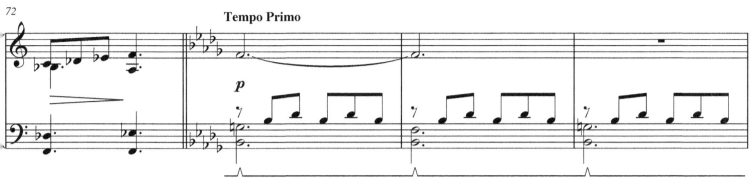

Tempo Primo

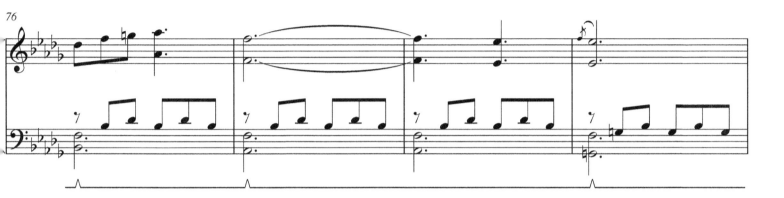

A Promise to Return

By Bear McCreary

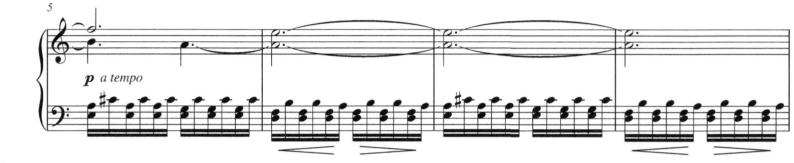

Allegro

By Bear McCreary

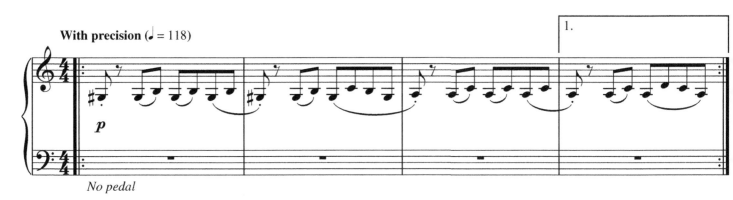

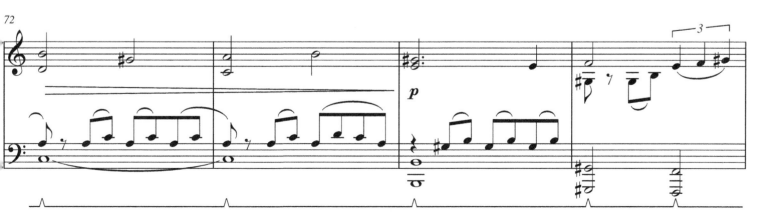

(no pedal)

Pegasus

By Bear McCreary

Moderato (♩ = 75)

Prelude to War

By Bear McCreary

Aggressive, but not too fast (♩ = 118)

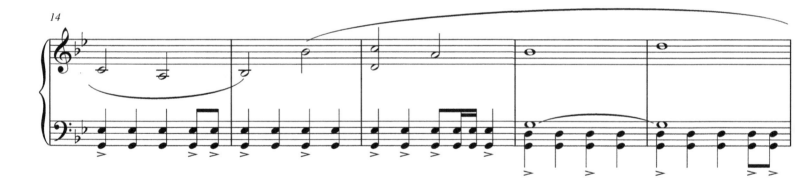

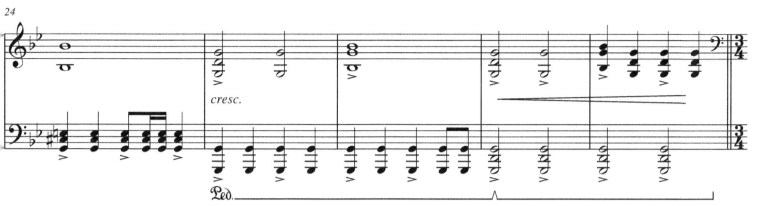

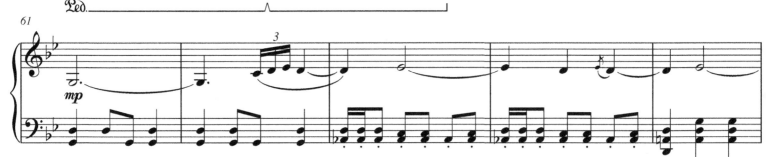

72

77

81

mf cresc. second time

85

f

89

ff (Percussive!)

93

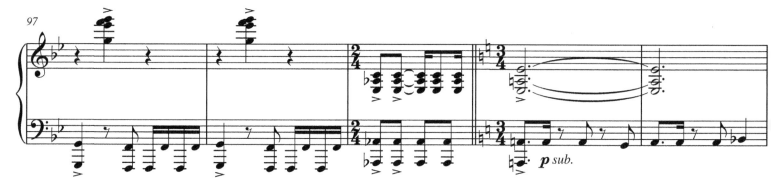

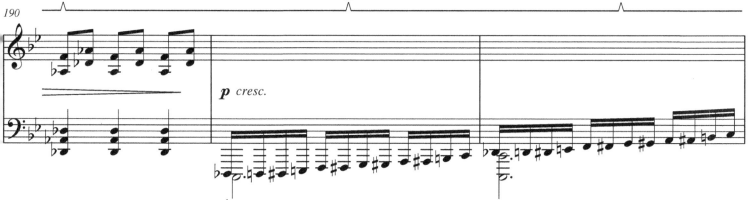

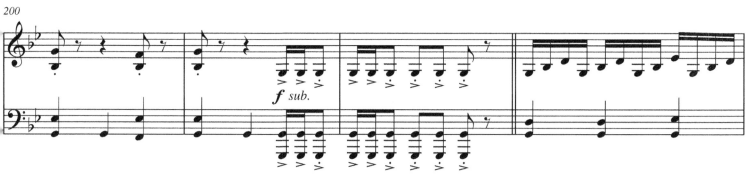

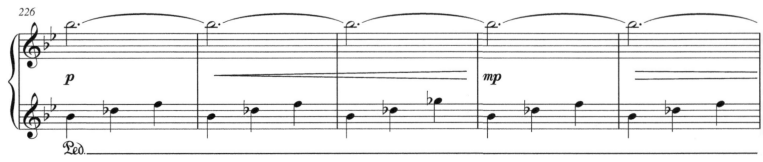

231

237

241

245
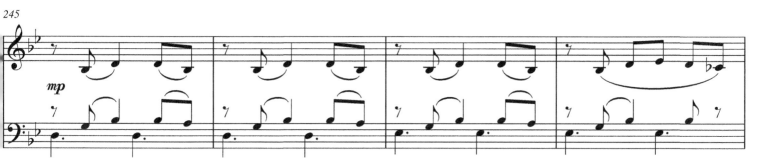

249
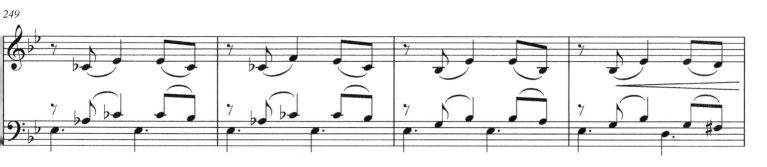

253
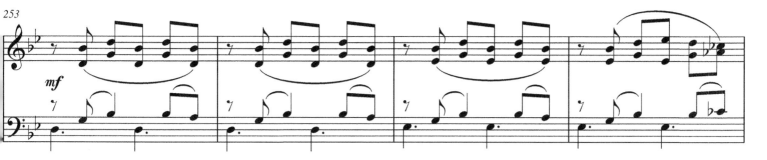

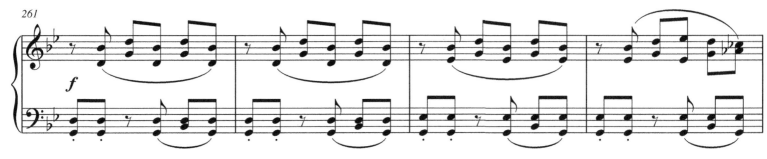

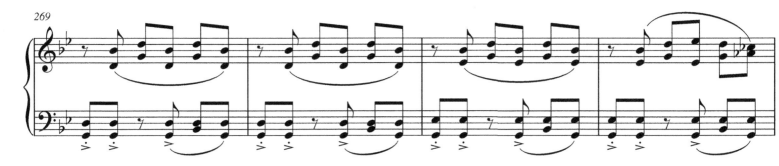

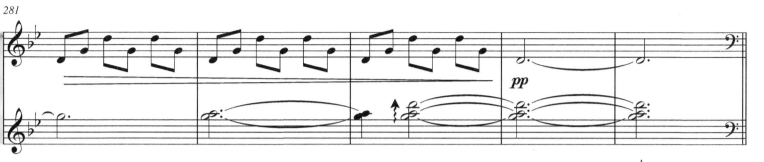

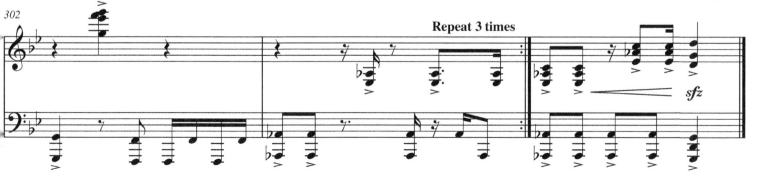

Worthy of Survival

By Bear McCreary

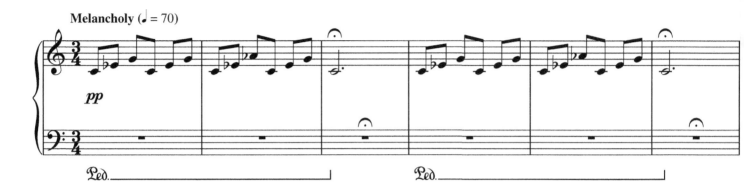

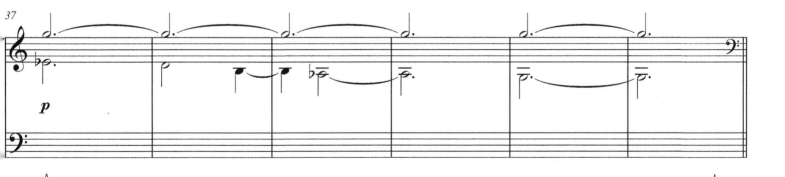

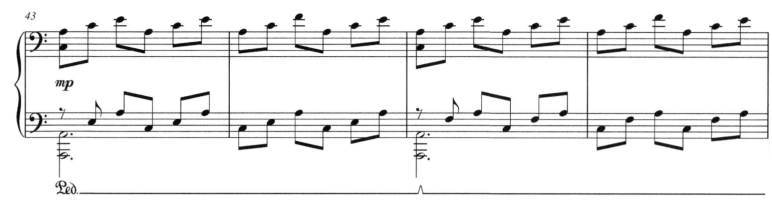

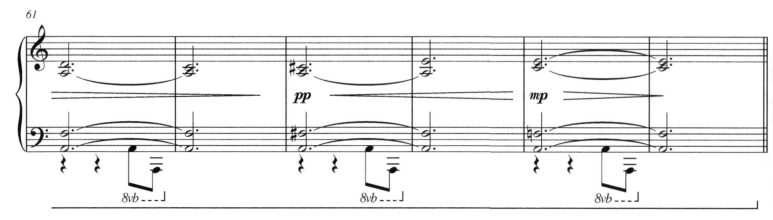

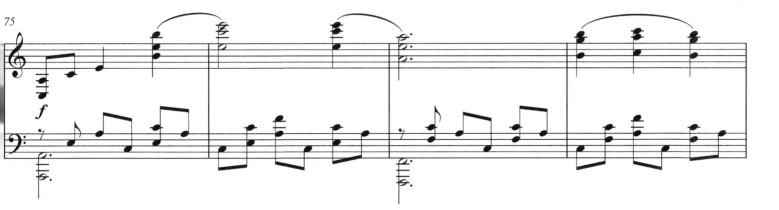

Something Dark Is Coming

By Bear McCreary

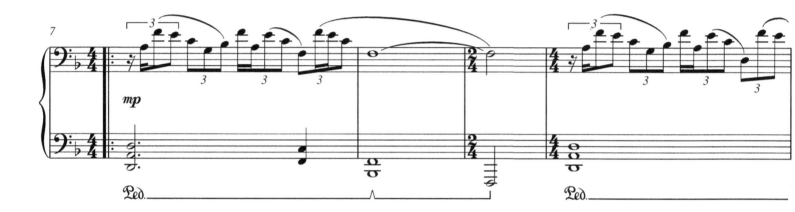

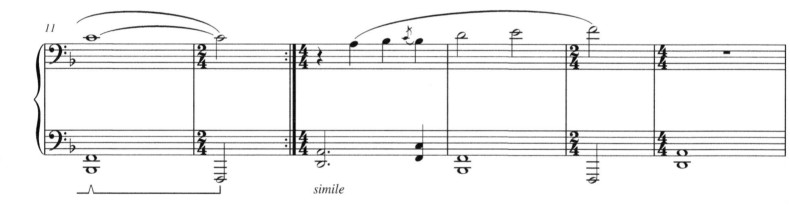

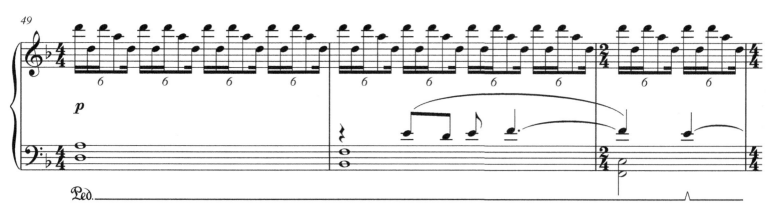

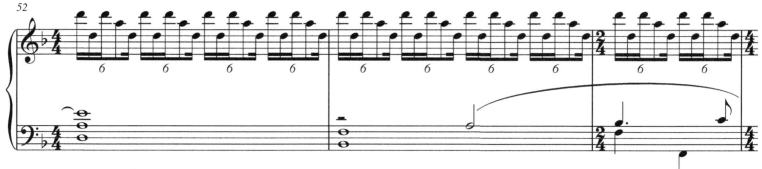

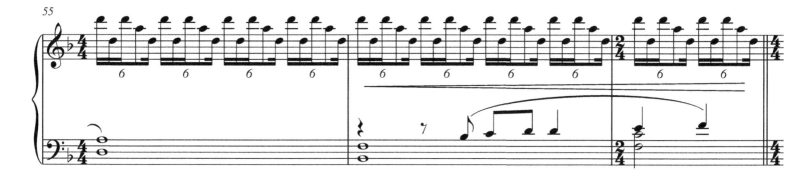

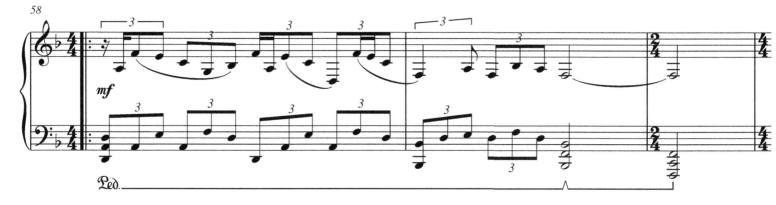

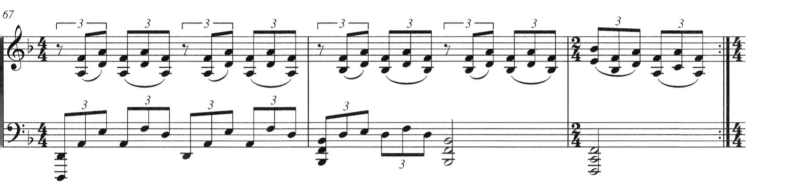

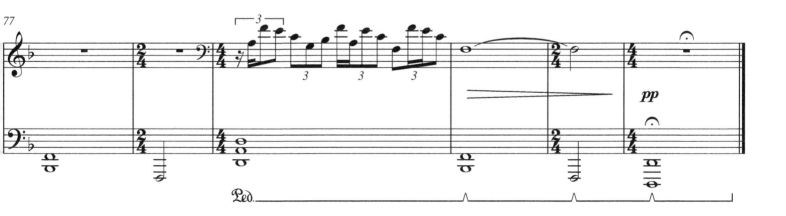

Violence and Variations

By Bear McCreary

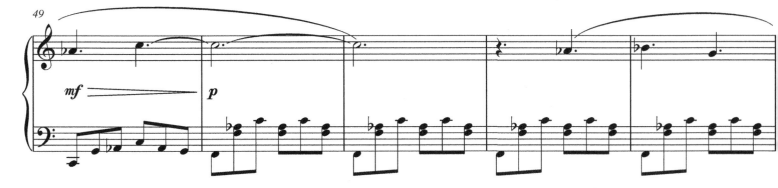

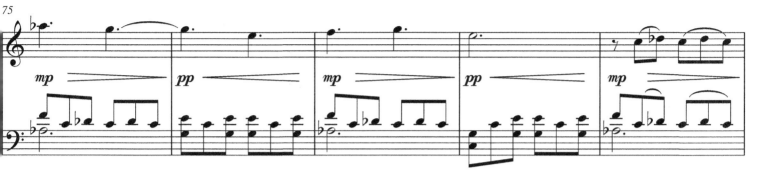

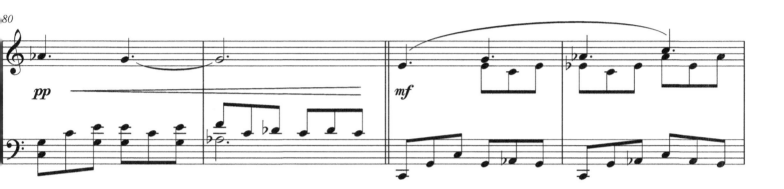

97 **Slower, but with more energy** (♩. = 44)

(no pedal)

100

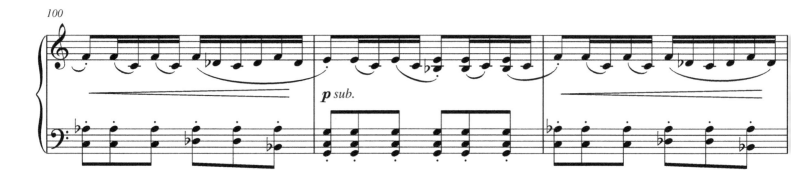

103

106

109

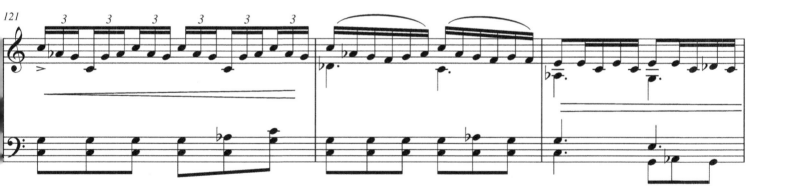

129

Faster (♩. = 66)

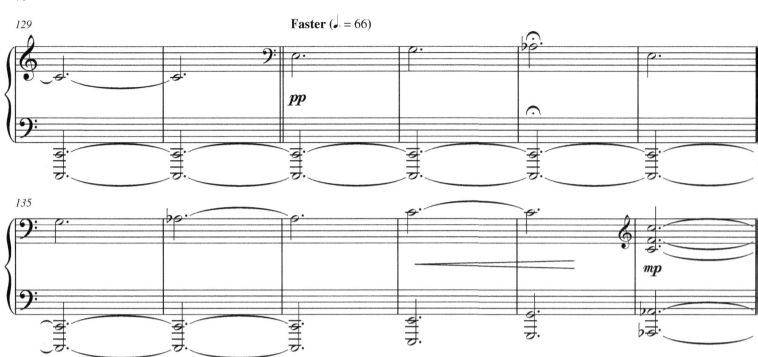

135

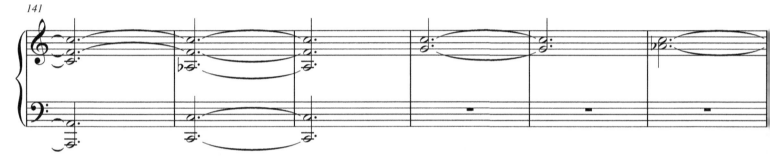

141

147

153

157

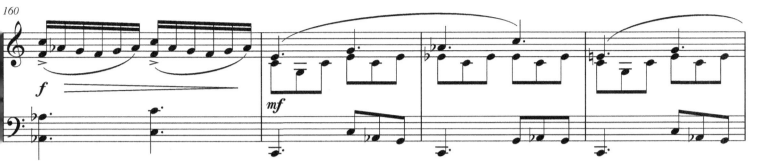

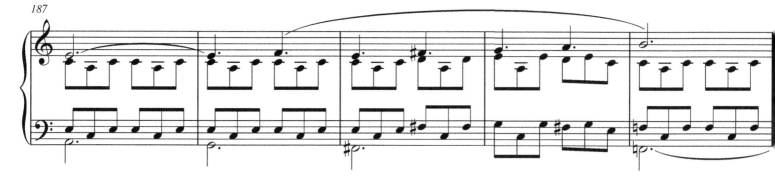

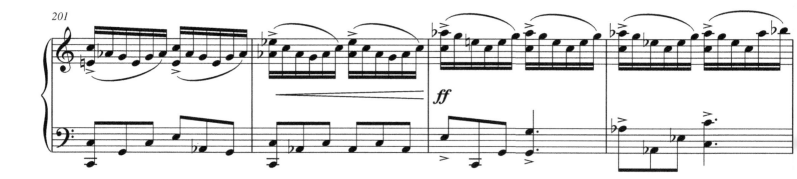

Resurrection Hub

By Bear McCreary

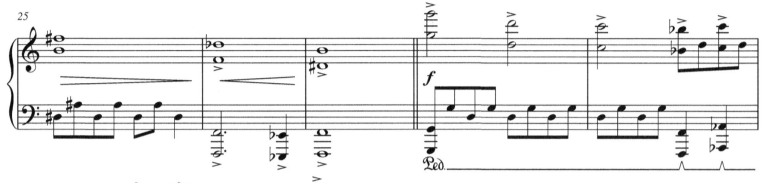

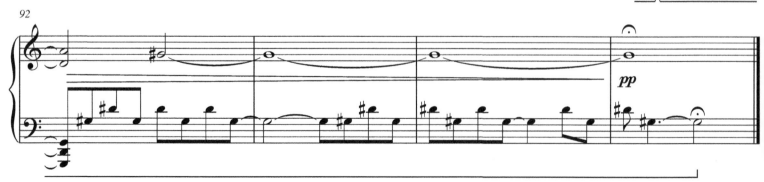

Apocalypse

By Bear McCreary

Freely, reverently

p

With light pedal

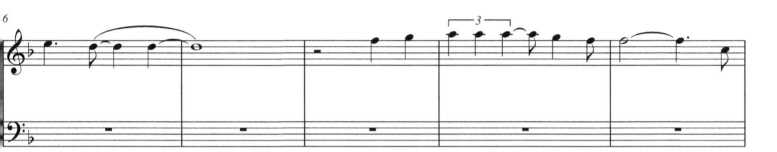

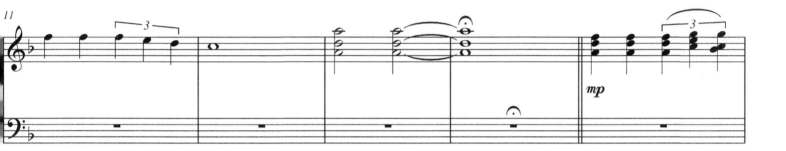

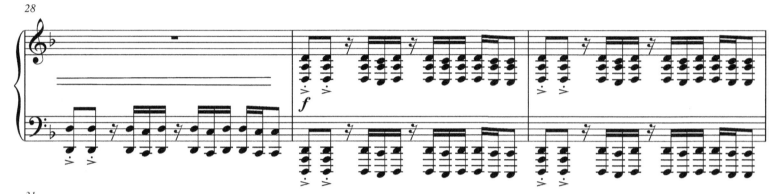

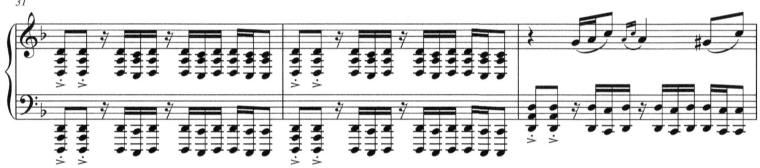

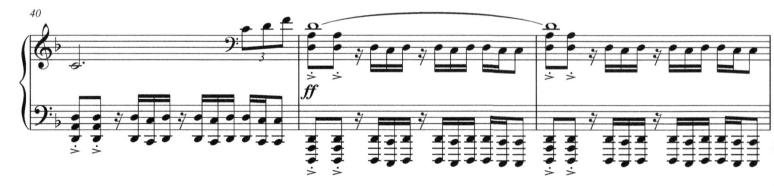

79

_____ simile

83

86

89

92

95

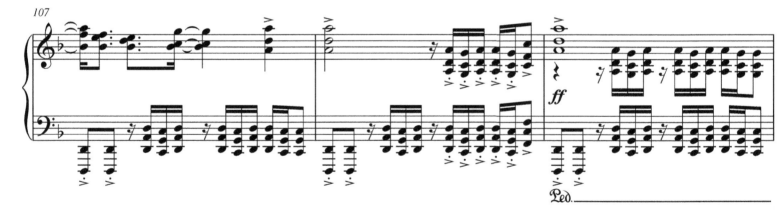

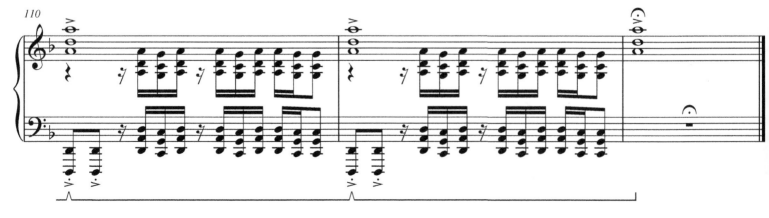

Battlestar Muzaktica

By Bear McCreary

Beyond the realms of good taste (♩ = 120)

mp

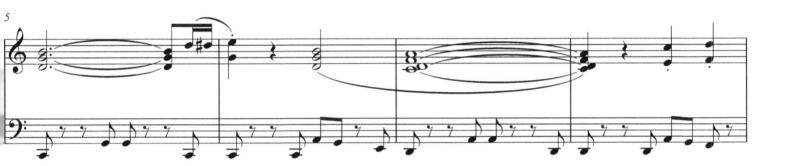

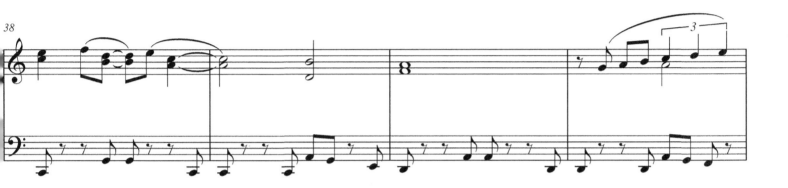

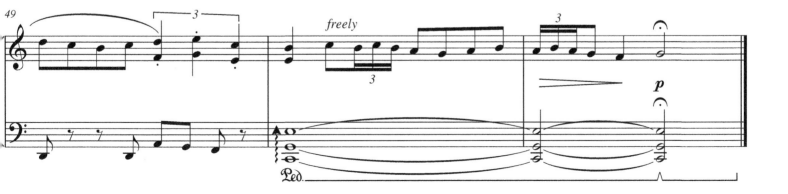

Roslin and Adama
Simplified Version

By Bear McCreary

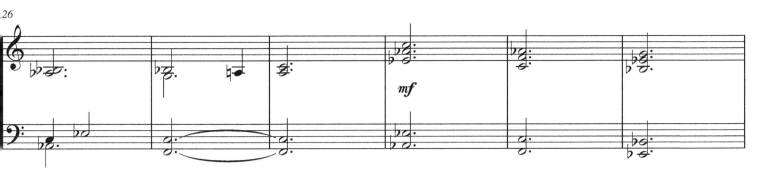

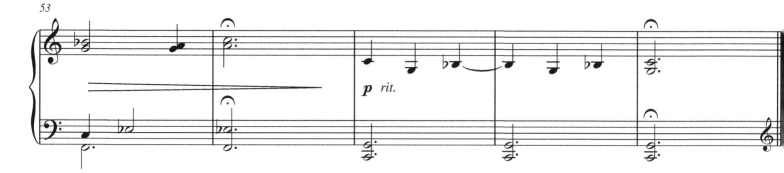

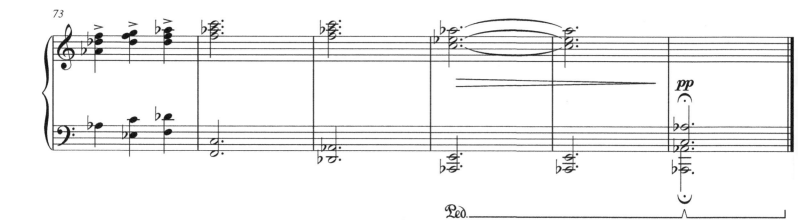

Wander My Friends

Simplified Version

By Bear McCreary

Moderato (♩ = 82)

p

Pedal freely

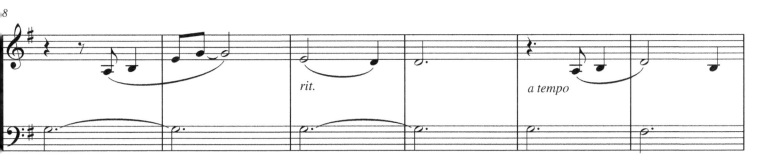

rit.

a tempo

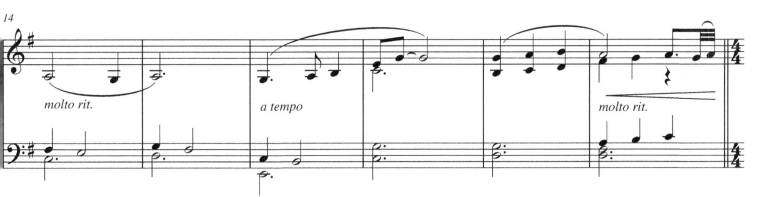

molto rit.

a tempo

molto rit.

Slower (♩ = 67)

mp

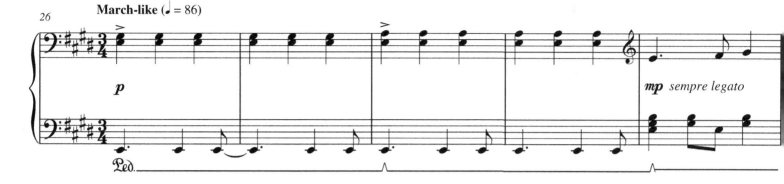

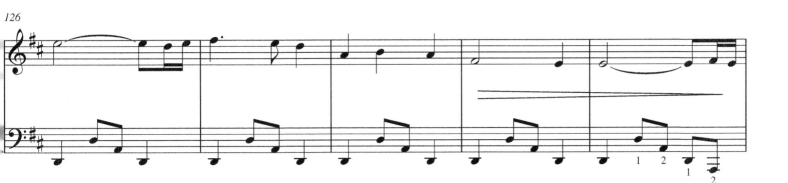

Kara Remembers

for one piano, four hands

By Bear McCreary

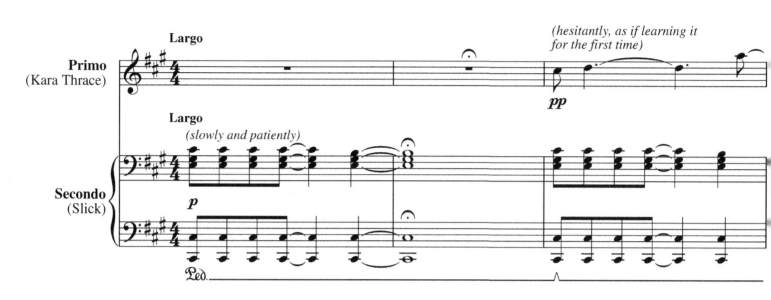

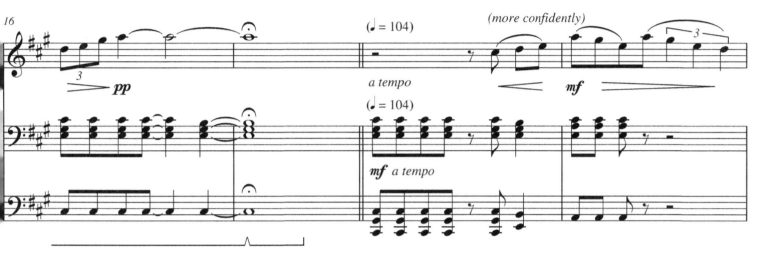

Battlestar Operatica

for Soprano and Piano

Words and Music by
Bear McCreary

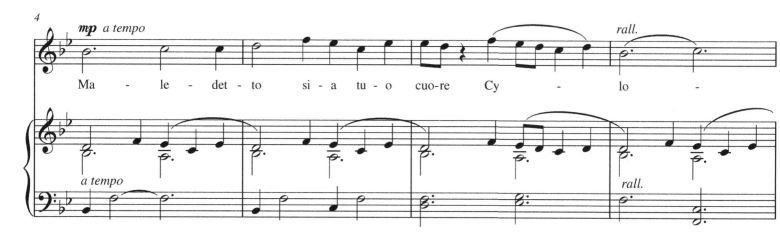

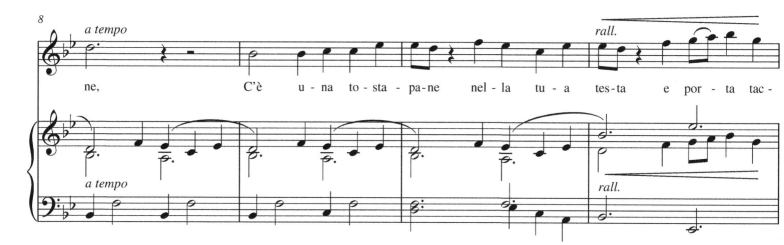

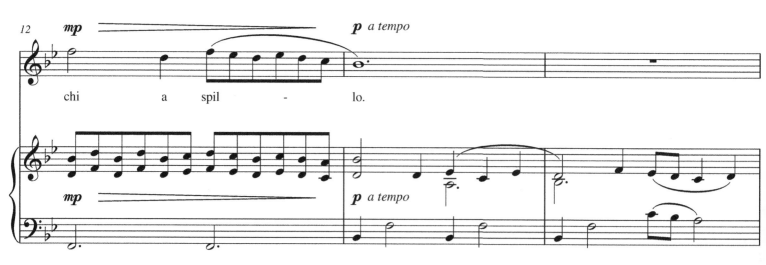

Nu - me - ro ___ Sei ti ___ chia - ma. ___ Il ri-

ve - la - to - re Cy - lo - ne im - po - ne la tu - a ra - gaz - za è un

to - sta - pa - ne. ___

Ma - le - det - to si - a tu - o

cuo - re Cy - lo - ne, Ahi - mè, Dis - gra - zia! Ahi - mè, Tri -

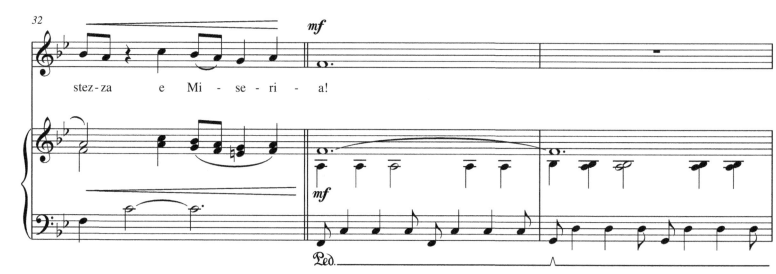

stez - za e Mi - se - ri - a!

Il to - sta - pa - ne ha un

bel ve - sti - to, Ros - so co - me la su - a

spi - na____ dor-sa - le ar - den - te sus-su - ra Nu-me-ro Sei: "Per____

tu - o co - man - do."

Ma - le - det - to si - a tu - o cuo-re Cy -

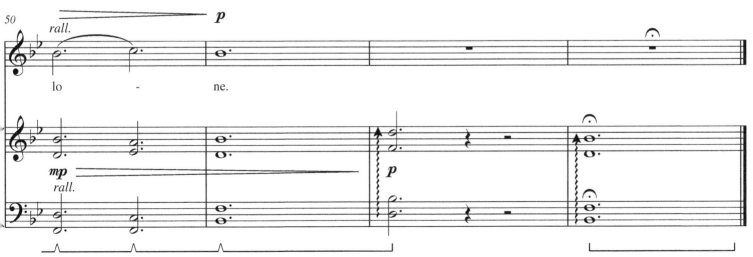

lo - ne.

BIOGRAPHY

Bear McCreary holds degrees in composition and recording arts from the prestigious Thornton School of Music at the University of Southern California. However, his professional training came from film music legend Elmer Bernstein, who taught him the tools of the trade. By the age of 24, McCreary was launched into pop culture with his groundbreaking score to SyFy's hit series *Battlestar Galactica*, for which he composed "the most innovative music on TV today" (*Variety*). It "fits the action so perfectly, it's almost devastating: a sci-fi score like no other" (NPR). *Io9.com* declared Bear McCreary one of the Ten Best Science Fiction Composers of all time, listing him alongside legends John Williams, Jerry Goldsmith and Bernard Herrmann.

McCreary's many other credits include the worldwide smash-hit series *The Walking Dead*, where he collaborated with writer/director Frank Darabont (*The Shawshank Redemption*). He has also composed critically-acclaimed scores for series such as *Terminator: The Sarah Connor Chronicles*, *Caprica*, *The Cape* and *Eureka*. His swash-buckling score for *Human Target* featured the largest orchestra ever assembled for a television series in history, and earned him his first Emmy® nomination for Outstanding Main Title Theme. His feature film work includes Disney's *Step Up 3D*, and his videogame credits include "SOCOM 4" and "Dark Void."